CW00404474

SHEET-ANCHOR

Trevie

Sheet-Anchor

PRISCILLA NAPIER

With a Foreword by
ERIC LINKLATER

THE ERSKINE PRESS
2000

Sheet-Anchor

First published in 1944 by
Sidgwick and Jackson Limited
This edition published in 2000 by
The Erskine Press, The Old Bakery, Banham, Norwich, Norfolk NR16 2HW

ISBN 1 85297 064 2

British Library Cataloguing-in-Publication Data
A catalogue record of this book is available
from the British Library

Printed in England

CONTENTS

INTRODUCTION

Priscilla Napier published this book towards the end of the War and at that time it appeared under the pseudonym of Eve Stuart. Accordingly the name 'Michael' was substituted for that of her husband, Trevie Napier, throughout the first edition. But with the passage of time she felt less strongly about the need to preserve this anonymity and allowed Eric Linklater to use their real identities when he included his Foreword to *Sheet-Anchor* in a book of essays on 'The Art of Adventure' (Macmillan 1947). I have therefore decided to use the real names in this edition.

The production of *Sheet-Anchor* by Sidgwick and Jackson was fraught with problems. It was delayed firstly by wartime restrictions on the amount of paper available for printing and then by postponement of the binding process 'due to enemy action'. But a small edition was finally completed in 1944 earning enthusiastic reviews and much praise. The book sold out quickly with the result that only a very few much thumbed and greatly treasured copies now remain in the family.

Priscilla Napier died in 1998 at the age of 90. Since her death a volume of her shorter poems has been published entitled *Coming Home from Sea* (Erskine Press, 1999), and this included several major extracts from *Sheet-Anchor*. This small book contains *Sheet-Anchor* in its entirety, complete with the original Foreword by Eric Linklater, and is for the many readers of her other books and of her poetry who have asked to see it.

More especially this book is for Priscilla Napier's grandchildren who greatly loved and admired her, and for her great grandchildren who in their turn will come to value *Sheet-Anchor* not only for the power of the writing but for its evocation of the courage, vision and selflessness of those who, in the prime of life, were caught up in so momentous a time of war.

LAVINIA ROBINSON 2000

There are in English literature a number of poems which celebrate the beloved dead; Milton's 'Lycidas', Tennyson's 'In Memoriam', very much of Housman's work were notes struck by the blow of abstract grief from the metal of the human soul. It is not claiming too much for *Sheet-Anchor* to say that it is of this illustrious company.

Country Life

Sheet-Anchor, a group of poems to the memory of a naval officer by his wife, transcending the personal and immediate, is a memorial to courage itself. '... Among men, as among pictures,' writes Eric Linklater in his Foreword to the book, 'there are masterpieces, and he was one.' The poems are worthy of their subject.

The Times Educational Supplement

Sheet-Anchor is a poem which can be appreciated but not criticised, for it is written in memory by the wife of a naval officer who died in the war, and because such sorrow is holy ground, because of its fierce sincerity, one does not readily speak. There is in it a triumphing persuasion of faith in the eternal quality of love.

Western Morning News

Sheet-Anchor is in a class by itself. The long introduction by Mr Eric Linklater is in itself admirable, and introduces us to the subject of the chief poem in the book, 'To Trevie, Dying'. Its author has written something that might easily have toppled over into bathos, but it never does. Her poem is a fast moving tribute to her husband, whose fine qualities seem to have inspired equally fine creative powers. No one could read her book without feeling spiritually enriched.

The Scotsman

The poems wring out of the pain of a heroic death, imaginatively comprehended, a reality that kindles the spirit to commit itself more generously to life. The verse throughout is of a compelling and lyrical eloquence.

The Times Literary Supplement

Remarks and comments following the publication of the 1944 edition by Sidgwick & Jackson

FOREWORD

BY ERIC LINKLATER

Trevie, the subject and inspiration of these poems, was a Naval Officer who died on duty, and of his duty, in the late summer of 1940. The author of the poems is his wife.

The last time I saw Trevie was in October 1939, when for a day or two his ship lay at moorings behind a little, flat-topped, heathery island at the entrance to Scapa Flow. Earlier in the month I had watched him coming into harbour with a couple of other destroyers and a pair of cruisers, a wild south-easterly gale behind them and broken sunlight touching the grey sea with livid fingers. Spray rose in recurrent curtains over the cliff where my working-party was sandbagging a searchlight emplacement that clung to the rock like a fulmar's nest; and now and then, broken on a reef fifty feet below, the top of a wave rose angrily, solid water with enough weight in it to knock a man off his feet. Even on land the sea was dangerous, and in the Sound below it was elemental fury: white-hooded ridges impending over darker gulfs; great shouldering waves, tatter-crested, running in a ponderous destructive rhythm that would have made a charge of elephants seem, in comparison, a feather-footed *pas de ballet*.

The warships came in, riding with an apparently reckless mastery the procession of the storm—now with a roll rising bow-in-air, now lurching in a smother of white water through the wave

1

before—and turning hard to port took the weight of the sea on their sides. The cruisers rolled so steeply that we on the cliff could see their whole decks as if we were looking down at a plan of them, but the destroyers were more nimble, more dexterous, and with a marvellous dashing assurance found their footing quickly in those treacherous valleys, and sped easily in towards the opening boom. They were very beautiful in their narrow strength and fleet design.

They had been on duty since the middle of August. A nervous duty, taut and sleepless, for we were ill-prepared for war and on the destroyers, patrolling the outer lines of our defence, a heavy burden lay. At the outbreak of war the Home Fleet anchored in Scapa Flow, and in September of 1939 Scapa was thinly guarded by a few hundred local Territorials, by a little cluster of anti-aircraft guns, a few elderly pieces of coast artillery, and some vestigial booms that nowhere closed the sounds they were supposed to lock. The insufficiency of these defences was soon exposed, but while they were being strengthened, while all our terrifying weaknesses were slowly fortified to meet the crisis of the following year, the Royal Navy had to watch the piquet-lines from Arctic ice to Channel fog and far into the grey pampas of the deep Atlantic; and show no consciousness to the enemy, nor admit it to themselves, of the frailty they enclosed.

Day after day, from our small Orcadian island, we saw the King's ships go out, the white ensign brilliant against the blue and gold of autumn skies and ripened corn, or wrenching from the staff in a northern gale. We saw them come home again, shadows in the darkness, and in the morning, it might be, the flanks of a destroyer that we knew were pocked by gunfire, a battleship lay as if weary with one side lower than the other, and a cruiser, tenderly escorted, was slowly coming up the Sound with its stern under water. Many chapters of gallantry, of valiant defence and superb attack, will have to be written to make a true and proper history of this war, but no splendour of arms, by land or sky, may dim . the memory of the duffle-coated men who, with efficiency that had no peer at that time, with the same derisive grin for the enemy's pretence and their own misfortune, with the quiet and seemly fortitude of their profession, waged their unchronicled invisible war from Bear Island to the tall Azores. How often we of the garrison, in those first twelve months, said or heard, in the jesting tone that concealed a knowledge too grim for plain admission, 'Thank God we've got a Navy!'

In a letter dated in September Trevie wrote: 'We are almost always at sea. Some figures at the end of this trip are four complete days in harbour in the last forty; one in the last eighteen. One night out of my clothes, of four hours' duration, out of eleven; and so on. We keep very well on this. In the opinion of the ship's company we have sunk four submarines, and certainly I can't disprove it. Personally I think it likely enough we have got two, but the Lord knows.'

A few days later he was off the south-west coast of Norway. 'We had been going full speed all night, and as far as the destroyers were concerned had been drowned in heavy spray the whole time, a good deal of which had got below and amongst other things started to put the dynamos and electric installation out of action. It was as unpleasant and exhausting a night on the bridge as I remember.' Then the bombers arrived, and for about five hours the force of cruisers and destroyers was attacked from cloud-cover and the dazzle of the sun. This, in early October, was a new experience. Anti-aircraft gunners were in their novitiate, the guns themselves were limited to forty degrees elevation, and eyes were still untrained in the art of calculating the bright parabola of a falling bomb. They were anxious hours and then, when the attack was broken off, a gale blew up and at high speed through a dangerously heavy sea—rolling fiercely, everything in the ship awash—they set their course for Scapa, and after fourteen days at

3

sea spent their first night in harbour with steam on all engines and a prayer that the wind wouldn't shift; for the anchorage was closely crowded, and every ship, in the wild darkness, was yawing eighty or ninety degrees.

Nor was there safety in Scapa. On October the thirteenth the German U-boat commander, Prien, came in on the top of the tide through a half-blocked sound and sank the *Royal Oak*. Four days later the Luftwaffe appeared in some strength, and in the first attack so badly shook the elderly bottom of the *Iron Duke* that she had to be beached. At intervals from half-past ten till nearly tea-time there were bombs falling, and the destroyers, now darting at sudden speed, now intently loitering, maintained with the shore batteries a hopeful bombardment. A Junkers came smoking down on Hoy; another, badly wounded, went fluttering away to the east, and a Tribal hoisted the complacent signal, 'My bird, I think.'

One day I went to lunch with Trevie, and hardly had I gone aboard when another raid-warning came in. I followed Trevie to the bridge. In a few seconds the ship had come to life like a bee-hive when you strike it with a stick; but more quietly, far more quietly. Trevie gave his orders in so soft and easy a voice that I could scarcely hear them—in the very tone of a friendly, rather idle man murmuring to a neighbour, 'It's going to be warm to-day,'—yet on the instant, on the very point of the instant, as it seemed, the cable was slipped, we were under way, suddenly moving at great speed, and every gun was manned and ready. The smooth efficiency of the ship made one think of the hard lubricated steel of a piston-rod, but far more amazing was a gentleness in the air. The small occasional mutter of conversation on the bridge was friendly talk, with perhaps half a joke to follow a helm-order or someone's comment on the scene. Discipline had come to very perfection, but that, after all, is no rarity in the Royal Navy; the remarkable thing about Trevie's discipline was that it looked like courtesy.

His habitual quietness in action was observed , with interest, by a more competent witness than myself: by a Naval Officer of senior rank and long experience who took passage with him when, in this same destroyer, he was escorting a convoy from Forth to Humber early in 1940. 'The passage,' he wrote, 'was made in almost continuous fog, the most exacting conditions which the captain of a convoy-escort destroyer can experience. We left Methil in visibility of two to three hundred yards, and met a big Dutch tanker bows-on almost directly after we started. A collision seemed inevitable, but we cleared the danger. I have been in perhaps scores of similarly narrow squeaks in my time, but I remember in that instant realizing that Trevie was giving the orders that saved his ship with a combination of tranquillity and unhesitating decision unique in my experience. This calmness was the keynote of the bridge by day and night.'

In such a tranquillity, then, we steamed here and there about the Flow, and presently returning to the mooring-buoy, went down again to lunch. We talked a little about the war, a little about our domestic affairs, and a great deal about men. About the sailors and soldiers, half-made as yet, on whose innocence an historical responsibility had suddenly descended. Trevie had no illusions about human nature, and yet was not only tolerant but hopeful of it. He had started the war with fifty seaman ratings, in a ship's company of rather more than two hundred, who had never been to sea before: in such circumstances a sanguine view of human capacity is hopeful indeed.

When he spoke of men who were clearly inefficient, there was neither surprise nor anger in his voice; of a good man, or a promising or unusual man, he would speak with the judicial warmth of a connoisseur. He was, I think, a connoisseur of men as other men are of wine: but not, of course, an idle connoisseur, for his mind was serious within its charm, and his whole life transparently purposive, 'his only avarice to serve.'

5

As a commander of men and ships he had native advantages. From a double line of Naval ancestors he had inherited the tradition of service and the gift of authority. He was very tall and lean, with fair hair growing thick and straight, a good face with strong but lightly moulded features. *Καλὸς κὰι 'αγαθός* I might have called him and been done with it, had I known him, not in Scapa, but the bay of Salamis; but nowadays we can be plain and unaffected only when we are recounting a man's vices, and grow embarrassed if we must say he is good and beautiful. Nor, in sober truth, would I have it otherwise, for there are subtleties in us that we should under-esteem if we dealt so simply with each other's virtues; and Trevie was not a simple character.

He was shy, and that, on the surface, is strange in a man so variously gifted and born to his profession as if it had been his father's estate; but one of the deficiencies that can make a man shy is lack of the common faculty of self-deception. Trevie was not guarded by complacency. With his conservative instincts went a radical mind, and the thought of injustice worried him like an old sore. 'I am the Red in my family,' he once wrote. At another time, from his sea-cabin, he analysed in detail the financial circumstances of women and children left, by the death of husband and father, to live on a Service pension; and with a scrupulous finger indicated, against a background of general hardship, the peculiar hardships incidental to the families of ratings, petty officers, and commissioned officers. He knew the life of a sailor, both at home and afloat, almost as well as his way into the Grand Harbour.

He was a humane man and troubled by it, but in the fashion of his kind he had acquired the constant habit of dissembling his feelings. When he felt deeply, he would speak lightly; he would deny or depreciate his own knowledge and ability; he would shun heroics as nimbly as he had avoided falling bombs, and seek immediate refuge from emotion in the shelter of a joke. In one of his letters he wrote of another officer: 'M.C. picked up the survivors of the ****** sunk in forty-five seconds, having previously avoided a torpedo himself by very adroit use of the helm, and delivered a heavy attack. The only part he tells anyone is that he was in the lavatory and the ****** had gone before he could do his trousers up, and how extraordinarily decent it was of the Senior Survivor not to be offensive to him about having to wait in the sea while he chased the submarine.'

This mannerism is a luxury which only men with a certain wealth of character may afford, that only men of a refined and curious sensibility will care to use. It is very nearly common form in the wardrooms of His Majesty's destroyers, and a variety of it used to be highly regarded in China.

I first met Trevie in Italy about ten years ago. While my wife and I were living there, he in a destroyer—his second command—lay briefly in a nearby port. He came to see us, and in the brilliancy of the Tuscan sun, against the ebullience of a dark loquacious people, he was so conspicuously, unmistakably, and completely English that one could hardly silence an exclamation of delighted recognition: the sort of exclamation one makes in a provincial art gallery when, among a score of pictures by agreeable but innominate Dutchmen one perceives, in its luminous certainty, an unquestionable Vermeer. The artist's signature was written clear upon him.

His talk that day was the light amusing gossip of the Navy in peace-time, when the blundering of some unfortunate junior officer and the idiosyncrasies of an admiral were culled and caressed and so lovingly preserved in anecdote that the listener was in some danger of thinking that charming misadventure and droll remarks were the normal routine of the Fleet. But later, when I went aboard his ship in the narrow-mouthed, tightly packed harbour, Trevie was more serious and spoke, as six years after on colder waters, about the sailors and the problem, new to the world, of how to feed and occupy and develop the minds of men who have been given the little education that does no more than create an appetite. They knew enough to be bored, and the Mediterranean, that provides the wardroom with plenty of amusement, could be boring indeed to the lower deck. Trevie was already searching for an answer to the question that has perplexed many able minds during this war that combines, with such monstrous inhumanity, so much sedulous care for humanity: the great question, What can we do to make other people's lives more interesting?

He could sympathize with boredom, for he had learnt its stale smell in the last war, when at sixteen he went to sea as a midshipman in a battleship of the Grand Fleet. For much of the time the Fleet lay in Scapa, waiting for the Germans to come out of Kiel, and a midshipman's life in an anchored battleship could be miserable enough. Later he saw some active service in the Baltic and the Black Sea, and in the years of peace there was long service in the Mediterranean, with early promotion and shore appointments of the sort that promised further advancement. He was destined, as it falsely seemed, for ultimate service in the highest rank, and his fellow-officers who foretold his success spoke of it with no envy in their voices, but with happiness in his prospects and confidence that his advancement would be the Navy's benefit. He might indeed have become an outstanding figure in Naval affairs, for he had a restless mind, a reformer's mind, and the practical ability as a seaman that would have made his opinion in other matters than seamanship respected. He had also the unstudied charm which integrity sometimes—not always indeed—wears like a bloom upon it, and that is a gift which gathers adherents and makes devoted friends for a very simple reason: it is good in itself, it is gratifying to be near and feel it.

That first winter of the war was rough and bitter-cold. Soldiers in their precarious lines in Northern France felt the violence of

8

the weather, and their difficulties became common knowledge. But when winter looks harshly on the land, it is roaring like a drunken savage on the sea. Ships in the North Sea, despite their internal heat, were often covered deep in frozen snow, and the spray that lashed them turned as it fell into solid ice. Trevie wrote: 'Things are sticky—hell! how I wish I could write freely—the last thirty-six hours have been the devil. I had better say nothing about the occupation, but we've spent it off a lee shore during the second and third days of a full S.E. gale, and even at the very slow speeds to which, rather to my anxiety, I have been forced to reduce, we have smashed the wardroom to atoms.'

That was in January. In February: 'We have had a hellish four days of unremitting S.E. gale, the last day with the biggest sea I have seen in the North Sea, and visibility about four hundred yards in a constant snowstorm.' His welcome, when he returned to harbour, was a letter from his bank complaining about a small overdraft.

And there was no rest, there could never be any rest, because destroyers were always needed, urgently and desperately needed, and neither great gales nor physical weariness could be counted against that need. In another letter Trevie wrote: 'I have been having eventful, wearing, anxious, and even stirring times. At the moment I am roaring round the ocean with a cruiser in four cables' visibility, blowing hard, because it is too thick to make the precarious land-fall of the desired haven, but every time we get halfway to an alternative it clears, and he thinks he ought to try again.'

That was immediately after the Norwegian campaign, in which Trevie's first duty had been to escort two small troopships from Aberdeen to Andalsnes. As everybody is now aware, there was a certain absence of preparation for that campaign, and Trevie's initial difficulty was that he had no proper chart of the Norwegian coast, and could not obtain one though he had to take his convoy fourteen miles up a narrow fjord. 'But I bought a railway map of Scandinavia in Newcastle, and it came in very useful,' he said.

On April the twenty-ninth he led a cruiser and another destroyer into Mölde Fjord. 'There has been very heavy bombing in there, and one can see clouds of smoke forty miles away. Very little hope of support from our air over here, but we will do what we can with our guns. I shan't mind when the party starts, but I hate these twelve hours or so of steaming quite steadily towards it.' Their mission was to take the King of Norway aboard.

Outside the fjord they were bombed but suffered no damage. And then: 'I led in at 20 knots, and as we opened out into the fjord we saw the town was in flames. As it got dark—as dark as it ever does here—the cruiser went alongside amongst the flames, and we patrolled to keep off submarines and M.T.B.'s. That was about ten. At twelve she signalled that the King was aboard, and that she intended to sail at once for Tromsö at 28 knots. Obviously a lot depended on how far we could get clear by daylight, and just as she was about to shove off, we heard the sound of aircraft overhead, then saw tracer bullets coining down, the cruiser firing, and two bombs drop. There was a tense moment as she was illumined by the flames. A few seconds later we heard a more personally threatening sound, and a great two-engined plane came whizzing down low over us at tremendous speed, machine-gunning us while our pompom blazed away, its tracers rushing upwards. A minute later it did it again. I think we were close to him. Then the cruiser appeared, coming after us, and I led out in the semi-darkness through the ten-mile length of rocky channel, this time at twenty-eight knots. Something in peace-time to turn one's hair grey. We were clear of the channel by two. It will be daylight at four. Did they guess the King was there? ... 10.30. Perhaps not, for we have got a good way now, and they haven't appeared though we are not out of range yet. At Namsos and Mölde it's still going on. Ashore in each is the base HQ of a force, and lying-off a little escort vessel with 4-inch HA guns to act as anti-aircraft defence and a wireless-link. They have the hell of a time. They are bombed all day and all night; and gradually run out of ammunition. ... 7 p.m. 30th. Here we are in the Arctic Circle, a most delightful place, warm and sunny and calm, with strange birds. To-morrow I am to go on and make the difficult passage into Tromsö and see if I can find a pilot for the cruiser. It is very peaceful out here after Mölde.'

The campaign came to its inglorious end, and news of our evacuation filled him with 'shame, rage, and horror. I wish the Government and the Press wouldn't pretend that this is not a disaster, and one largely brought about by our own incompetence,' he wrote. 'But the performance of the Fleet was excellent, though its use was futile, and I have acquired a profound respect for some of our soldiers.'

About mid-May he described his own situation as 'alarming, anxious, and exhausting, but not without interest. A contest has been in progress between ****** and myself and four or five bombers, lasting about two hours and proving that if conditions are good and if the destroyer has got freedom of movement, he can put a high-level bomber off his shot nearly every time by ship-handling. I have only had one night in, in sixteen, and we aren't done yet. Nothing at all on the horizontal in the last four nights, so I am feeling rather part-worn.'

The references to fatigue become more frequent as the summer's crop of disaster ripens, and the fears that no man escaped in that year sometimes show themselves in his letters like a bared nerve. Writing to his wife, in a seemingly calm paragraph about France's collapse and the possibility of America's intervention, he suddenly exclaims: 'Do you know how to put my gun together? Anyone will show you.' There was in his mind the knowledge that if England was successfully invaded, he would have to abandon his wife and children, and take his ship across the

11

Atlantic to continue the war from Canada. But suddenly as the fear came, comes a little domestic joke: 'I can imagine Aunt F—— being over-run by Italians, but not by Germans.' And then, with no more warning, his voice grows blunt and angry, and there is an explosion of injured patriotism: 'I hate all this blaming of ourselves; if other countries had done as much for the common good as we have in the last twenty years, the millennium would have arrived.'

His base, at this time, was Harwich. E-boats had become a greater menace than the Luftwaffe, for whose ragged inconclusive attack—ill-aimed bombing from a safe height—he was acquiring an irritated contempt. It robbed him of sleep when he was in harbour, and sleep was what he craved. He was by now ill indeed, though he would not admit it, but he still found time to write at great length, with heat and tireless inquiry, about Naval strategy, prospects in the Mediterranean, and the seemingly inevitable German invasion: 'I shall not waste my time crumpling my bows on an old barge. When I have expended my very considerable stock of ammunition and my torpedoes, I am by no means at the end of my resources for this sort of thing. I know one feels these chaps are so clever there is nothing they cannot do, but at sea one frequently comes across things which they *can't* do.'

He was quite sure that the Germans would invade, or try to, and he was determined to be there to meet the attack. That was why he would not leave his ship though he was continually tired, his legs were sore and stiff, and he grew so lame that he found difficulty in getting up to the bridge. 'It is no use resting through the invasion in order to feel more energetic during the occupation,' he wrote, and by a harsh and relentless discipline his indomitable will drove an exhausted body back to work and back to sea. Gentle to others, tolerant of frailty in another man because he knew that no man is without his weakness, he was merciless to himself, there was no loophole by which he might escape from his own conception of duty. And so this private war continued, of the spirit and the flesh; he waited from hour to hour for the Luftwaffe and the German landing-barges, and went to sea for the last days of his life with his mind harried by mortal sickness.

In mid-July he went ashore in a town on the East coast where there was a doctor whom he knew and trusted, and for that reason dared not visit. The ship's surgeon had been trying to persuade him to go on leave, 'but awaiting invasion at half an hour's notice,' said Trevie, 'how the hell can I walk into D.[1] and say I am run down and want a fortnight's sick leave? It is, of course, impossible with the ship in full running order, and no specific complaint. A good cold gale would be as good for me as anything, I think.'

Nor did he ever leave his ship of his own volition, but presently was carried off, and a few weeks later died. What he died of was septic endocarditis, which is the invasion of the heart by a specific organism that produces, at first, the appearances of any febrile disorder, and then, with no particular symptoms, increasing illness and finally prostration.

Among captains of ships in war-time, septic endocarditis is an occupational disease, an effect of unceasing strain.

When I undertook to write this memoir, I had not intended that it should be so long. It had been decided that a prefatory note, giving some facts about Trevie as I knew him, would be a useful introduction to his wife's poem; the poem itself, with its unashamed and noble passion, with a beauty that gathers its effect (like a choir of many voices) from a host of comely lines, needs nothing of my commendation, but because it is anonymous, and so detached, it was thought that I should serve as a kind of anchor for it. And this I was glad to do. But I could not do it as briefly as I had first expected, because in five hundred words I was unable to say what, with more thought, I wanted to say.

[1] The captain commanding a flotilla of destroyers.

13

I wanted, to be plain about it, to praise the Royal Navy, which can never be praised enough—I mean that part of it which goes to sea—and much of whose hard, unspectacular, essential and unceasing work is scarcely praised at all, because from the land it is invisible; and like the keeper of a provincial art gallery, drawing a visitor's attention to his Vermeer, I wanted to draw attention to Trevie, for the good reason that among men, as among pictures, there are masterpieces, and he was one.

In the anonymity of the poem, moreover, I found a bitter reminder that very many, who have died in this war and all wars, are nameless now except in official records and the brief remembrance of their friends; and we, who may wear our names a little longer, do so by their courtesy, and should in courtesy remember the purpose for which they died. 'Virtue has never won outright.'

TO TREVIE

1. EASTER, 1939

2. COMING HOME FROM SEA

3. RETURNING TO SEA

1. EASTER, 1939

This is for ever,
These unlit beech trees leaning over Teviot's stream,
Where you, with rod and boat,
High in reflected tree-tops float—
Figures in some absurd, celestial dream—
Over the river running emerald deep:
These distant shallows whose sweet roar comes faint,
This ceaseless, silly, innocent complaint
Of lambs crying to their mother sheep;
These primrose leaves unwrinkling at my feet,
This child with eager hand
Tirelessly drawing patterns in the river sand;
And the red field green-shadowed with young wheat,
This holiday, this love,
This Easter sun above,
This carelessness, this peace,
This heavenly springing of the earth's increase.

This has no finish, no catastrophe,
And death's disruptive hand
Cannot blot out these pictures in the sand,
This is for ever,
And no ephemeral headlines we may see

Screaming their deathly sentences abroad,
No shock, no agony of spirit, can sever
This timeless moment from the spread of time,
Though war unsheathe her adamantine sword
And howling dogs run free.
That noise, that tremor has no potency,
Those tortures will grow shadowy and pale,
This love, this moment of spring, was all our tale,
This orchestra, this rhyme,
Not written in language of mortality.

2. COMING HOME FROM SEA

The arch of heaven narrows,
And night unbends the bow
That shot those glittering arrows
A million years ago:
Dark, dark, and still, that multitudinous burning,
The giddy firmament forgets its turning;
Alone we quicken and live, at your returning.

No wind about the mountains
The unviewed snow dishevels,
Time holds the tumbling fountains
Fast frozen in their revels:
The caracoling seas forbear to churn,
The singing stars their harmony unlearn;
Alone we live and move, for you return.

3. RETURNING TO SEA

Sing, nightingale, and summer birds arise,
To drown the recreant music of farewell—
The midnight dockyard where the blue light lies,
The moment when there is no more to tell,
The long look, and the brave anticipant eyes
While the sea waits, and the dark waters swell.

There will be spring again, the young leaf lent,
The blossom lavished, and the rose revealed,
The calm enormous star, the young bow bent
At evening in the cuckoo-calling field,
The squandered beauty that is never spent
And all the matchless wealth that summers yield.

The spring was ours: sorrow no more to lose
That long abundant summer of the heart;
Should we love's sharp eternity refuse
Because the end crowds in upon the start?
We were alive, we loved, now let us choose
To live as if we never had to part;

To love, and to relinquish love's possessing,
To feel the joy more instant than the pain,
All ardours of the greedy heart addressing

Towards that past incomparable gain,
And from the fountain of remembered blessing
To drink the stream, and never thirst again.

TO TREVIE, DYING

TO TREVIE, DYING

I

Mortal affection, that on earth is given
As dear allegiance as man's heart can render,
Wan viceroy to the sovereign love of Heaven
Yet still the true reflection of its splendour,
Your noble diapason sound again:
Ring out, immortal tune! Till sorrow see
The stringent alchemy of love and pain
Compound her solace and antiphony,
And other lovers find
The undeterred, unfrustrate spirit of mankind.

This is the spirit's war, the breathless hour
While summer hangs her softness on the night,
Nothing but faith confronts the extreme of power,
And death is loosed; black harbingers of spite
With envious squadrons rip the evening veil,
Avenging lights in scintillant display
Arrow the firmament with questing flail;
Bofors and Oerlikon, their mounting spray
An angrier red than Mars
Spangle the vault of heaven with their transient stars.

This is the spirit's war, whether at sea
An icy vigilance through winter's roar
They keep, or gripped in sharp expectancy
Visit the verge of Norway's nightless shore,
Or high aloft, rare partisans that reach
The quicksilver vendettas of the sky,
Or stubborn on Dunkirk's immortal beach,
Casual, heroic, for one purpose die;
Through all dissatisfaction
Self-banished exiles from the blaze of youth and action.

Scarce-armed protagonists whose forfeit youth
Must now its utmost quality expend,
Who in the desperate pass of threatened truth
A wearier Thermopylae defend:
This shall be sung, this shall be sung with Troy,
The spur and stimulus of later fame,
While there are hearts to hear, shall tongues employ
The sorrows and the splendours of their name,
Whose hardihood set free
A fairer Helen from a worse captivity.

What is achievement? What resounding years
Echo accomplishment as fine as this?
This quiet derisive gallantry that clears
Honour that no oblivion can dismiss.
Envied adventurers, with no reward
Save singleness of mind in such a strife,
Who took the sword to perish by the sword,
Who hazarded their deeply valued life,
Who went with a mocking heart
And find in legend's tale no braver counterpart.

They set their course unstirred by trumpets' playing,
Or patriot's din, or old imperial strain;
With certain eye and level wisdom weighing
The instant loss against far distant gain;
With rich affection that could still enclose
Our politicianed, bland, distempered world
Clutching its lack-love safety in repose
Whilst the wild flags of tyranny unfurled:
With their sweet life redeeming
Fools for new folly, knaves for yet more vicious scheming.

They who endured this waste and this unreason,
This dull and brutal cancelling of hope,
Behaved with faith through all this fog of treason,
Knew the compelling light for which we grope.
This is unfaith—the penury of spirit,
The ignorance, the Pilatry, the sloth,
The long degrading failure to inherit
Our hard-won throne of century-slow growth,
This freedom, still a crown
Yearly re-won, lest inattention rust it down.

All that they saved is never safe,
The tyrant waves for ever chafe
On freedom's shore; justice and peace
Enjoy no durable release
From the betrayal of sloth and spite:
Virtue has never won outright.

All knowledge, all benignity,
All fiery truths that set men free
Are mortal, and their mortal spans
Depend on us; only in man's

Eternal willingness to die
To save them, does their safety lie.

Fortunate, whose live eyes behold
The evening hills aslope in gold,
Reject no more the sacrifice
That bought man's freedom at such price;
Love well, yours is the darling kiss
Free men forswore at Salamis;

Dare not to build with lesser pride
Sculptor for whom some Phidias died;
Or scorn the riches we inherit
From the long travail of man's spirit.
We are the action and the breath
Begot by all heroic death,

The compound and insatiate ghost
Of the crusaders' diverse host;
We are the phoenix purpose sprung
Out of the flame where saints were wrung,
The clear intent of those who fell
In the abyss of Passchendaele,

The vehement and continuing life
Of all who in the adamant strife
And crack of Jutland's cannonade
The sea engulfed; the undismayed
Strong winds of their ascending dove,
The mouthpiece of their matchless love.

II

Soft night, soft coolness of the evening quiet,
Sweet healing hand of summer and of sleep,
Stirred, murmuring trees, that past the instant riot
And tumult, their caressed perfection keep;
Aloof unravaged country for whose peace
A total happiness is well forsworn,
And splintered cities for whose far release
The torment and the loss is fairly borne—
For these the sternest pain
We do in full accept, and would accept again.

You that were strength itself are weakness now,
Stretched in long fever of the wearied heart,
You that with resolute and smoking prow
Endured through winter's rage the heaviest part;
You whom no clamorous seas could overleap,
The mounting waves of poison overwhelm ,
And fiercer tides to vaster oceans sweep
The rudder of your proud and steadfast helm,
Against whose vicious spate
With calm and mocking courage you yet navigate.

Not in the thunder and exhilarance
Of surface action wounded; but in these—
Perennial days of stony vigilance,
Interminable nights in the scorpion seas,
In the long roar of storm's besieging rumpus,
In the black minefields and the fog's eclipse.
Straining past mortal stature to encompass
The enormous ocean with the too scant ships,
On without sleep or rest
Till the worn flesh defaults before the will's behest.

You that are life itself draw near to death,
Life's very being fails, while the warm land
Murmurs and shines with summer's lavish breath;
The quivering oats are reaped, the corncocks stand,
And blue with afternoon, the slope hills run
Their feathered promontories in Tamar's gleam,
The valleys mist and clear, the glowing sun
Lights the curved haunches of the reaper's team,
And evening rings the cry
Of garrulous homing rooks, night-blown across the sky.

A comfort and a strength that never sleep
Delirium cannot change nor death disarm;
Even in this extremity you keep
Each weapon in your armoury of charm:
Kind hands, the gentle and deliberate voice,
The matchless smile, the blue discerning eyes,
Such lordly looks as most the heart rejoice
And did my mind long since emparadize,
Who wore in your brief span
Bearing and truth to vindicate God's hopes of man.

O strong ambassador from God, who held
His richest gift, the understanding heart,
And lively mind whose openness expelled
The narrow rivalries in which men smart,
Whose interest and sympathy were keys
Of laughter, that unbars the guarded mind,
The lubricant of toil, division's ease,
Laughter that is affection, that is kind;
By the heart he dies
Whose province was the heart's continual exercise.

Bitter progression to an unseen end!
Thus, ever thus, the sovereignest heart must bleed,
The dearest lover his steps soonest bend
To Heaven, his soul from bravest body freed.
Were you that archangelic Michael sent
From armed etherial companies of Heaven
To fight this truest war, you had not spent
More faithfully your life, nor could have given
A fierier energy,
A nobler surety that man's spirit should be free.

Wisdom and strength are streaming from the earth,
Burning away in unavailing fight,
Laughter and friendship, truthfulness and mirth,
Are vapoured up into the hood of night;
All judgment, and all seamanship, all skill,
All coolness, all command and enterprise,
And all the sturdy qualities that fill
Men's hearts with reassurance. Spent he lies,
Whose courage could not swerve,
Whose greed was love, whose only avarice to serve.

Burning away the folly and disdain
Of England to herself too long untrue,
The shame of China, and the shame of Spain,
The Ethiop treachery, the hounded Jew—
Flower of our blood that can alone unwrite
The long betrayal of the inter-war,
When England still condoned the tyrant's might,
And free, her brother's liberty forswore—
Burning away in fee
For Munich's signing and Bohemia's slavery.

Burning away from summer and from light,
Away, away, from unaccomplished good,
Far from this battle that he longed to fight,
From all he guarded, helped, and understood;
See, see, their banishment—love's noontide blaze
And long serenity, the sweet parade
Of fireside joys, the hill and garden days
With sunny lawns and orchards flecked with shade
Or sprayed with April foam,
The cheerful liveliness of children and of home.

Whatever comfort waits, it is not this:
This suckling paradise of you-and-me,
This kindergarten love whose narrow bliss
Shutters the world from out its sanctuary.
What comfort in the chill angelic wastes
To set against this kingdom of rewards,
This lollipop affection that yet tastes
Joys more extravagant than Heaven affords,
This passion and this pleasure
Whose warmth the trudging years must now in bleakness
    measure?

Who is this eyeless creature, who is she,
Moving along the summer-gilded lane,
This breathing torment, walking agony,
Wrapped in a fog of frenzy and of pain?
I am God seeing, and I recognize
The fiercest pangs, the bitterest tears unshed,
I am the pain, and I am God that lies
Spent and immortal on the fevered bed:
This is a flash, a moment,
And I the timeless peace behind the present ferment.

Even at this, from some starred heavenly rafter,
Upon this rending agony of heart
We shall look back, we shall look back in laughter
At the impermanence of its brief smart;
All this will seem—even the year-long sigh,
The aching constancy of wild regret—
Diminutive and fleeting as a cry,
Sharp and immediate as an infant's fret
Whose now is his for ever,
Whom no proportioned judgment from his grief can
    sever.

You, that long ceased to pray the name of Christ,
Yet men called Christian—loving, true, and just,
Whose own entire endeavour well sufficed
To serve that God in whom you put your trust,
Whose courage and whose calm death cannot rout,
Who lie amused, irreverent, and unshriven,
Whilst all your strength and all your quietness shout
The glory and the certitude of Heaven,
Unchastened by pain's rod,
Proclaim the spinning and reverberate love of God;

All of yourself, all of your life proclaim,
All the compelling love by which you dealt,
Valour, integrity, and wisdom name
And praise that God to whom you never knelt;
The God that is the tempest and the turning,
Whom the resplendent firmaments declare,
The God that through the bitterness and burning
Discovers to the mind a joy more rare,
From love that seemed complete
Translates us to a rapture that is yet more sweet.

Too wildly loved, what stranger are you seeing
Looking at more than me? What foreign breath
Of haste invades your scorched and distant being,
And whence your power to ride the wrench of death?
This fortitude that holds the earth from shaking
From where translated, and what visions meet
Your dulling eyes, in that last victory making
Its only habitation in defeat?
Through whose extreme duress
Your speechless lips love's final verity express.

Death crowds on us, the fevers mount and gain
Above the clear vitality of youth,
Death bares his brazen countenance, makes plain
His strident and irrevocable truth.
Death cataracts about us, death is rife,
Devours the cities' splendours, drives his blade
With iron hardness through the heart of life,
And thunders his tremendous cannonade,
And fulminates above—
Yet there is nothing breathing in this room but love,

An excellence, love silent and alone,
A nakedness, a stripping of pretence,
Love seeking no reprieve, love as its own
Immediate and eternal recompense.
Duty and friendship are your full oblation
Who now, the entire and lavish service given,
Laughter and kindness your last consecration,
Discern that other country that is Heaven,
Whose soul, leaning towards bliss,
Asks no extremer unction than the lover's kiss.

The only hilltop whence we see
Is this prodigious calvary,
Solely through the gripe of pain
Will man discern the human plain,
Stripped by the wind of hate, discover
Mankind as his, himself as lover;

Diminished by each distant death,
Hungry in every famine's breath,
Heavy with that grim load the poor
Do universally endure,
By every servitude, unfree,
Abject in all men's misery.

Dullards, who only thus could learn
In London's fire, that all men burn,
Whom gelignite alone could teach
That the remotest Caspian reach
Is scarletted with our heart's blood,
Our darlings choke in China's flood.

For all we would not hear from Christ,
A hundred Messerschmitts sufficed
To teach us—that we love our brother,
That men are members of each other.
The good men tell us, year on year,
But only Heinkels catch the ear.

We yawn at crucifix and shock,
And all the ancient torments knock
Unheard upon the busied heart
Too dissipate to feel the smart,
We nail ourselves to other trees
Untaught throughout the centuries.

This darkness whence the bombs are hurled
This is the hunger of the world
Opening great mouths in London streets,
That with its crater jaws entreats
The bread of life—a part to bear,
From the earth's goods, a human share.

III

O freed of those twin tyrants, time and space,
The soaring spirit, whose unfettered mind
And soul's alacrity shall now embrace
Truth irrevealable to humankind!
Laugh, Trevie, in the merry courts of Heaven,
Stretch your long limbs upon the Olympian hills,
And skied flotillas from the planets seven
Enlist, while England still her charge fulfills:
Lean down, dear love, and yet
'Midst the massed cherubim afford a small regret.

You, always you, in the heart's country moving,
Whose mocking and inviolate life remains
In every thought and all conception proving
How strong a sovereignty the soul retains—
With fair tired head asleep beneath the tree,
In the true mind indomitably writ,
Proud on the bridge taking your ship to sea,
Seen past erasure and past counterfeit,
Engraved in more than stone,
Deep in the marrow of the soul unalterably known.

Joy is the native element of man
And happiness his circumfluent air,

Native the spring of jubilance whose span
Arches from childhood through the years' despair,
And pinnacles above the swamps surrounding
The desultory dwellings of our choice,
Its sudden jet continually astounding
Man's resignation with a silver voice
That through our desert birth
With affluent music pours its tributary of mirth.

Native as that unending faith we breed,
That deep insatiate appetite for good,
Strange purity in counsel and in deed,
That diverse and recurrent certitude
That virtue is the bread by which we live:
Native as that impassioned heavenward trend
By which we voyage, and in which we give
Our thankless labour for an unseen end;
That restlessness, that thirst,
Whose strength is the best hope on which mankind is
     nursed.

The planets wheel, the sun impervious spins,
The sullen centuries crowd their slow array,
The winters fume, the rampant spring begins,
Night coruscates for ever into day.
Time is unarmed, nor can disintegrate
With any wind from the deep zenith of space
This sealing body of love, nor separate
The scattered flesh from love's remembered grace,
The sense of coming home
Out of the wilderness in which our spirits roam,

That fountain love, incalculably springing
From the profound unmeasured lake of God,

Its clear renewal every morning bringing
A fresh delight in every pathway trod;
The sudden knowledge, the surprise of joy
In the mysterious tidings of a face,
That faith and certainty in the employ
Of love that is not virtue but is grace,
That loss whereon we thrive,
That headlong death of self, by which we come alive.

Before, before God lit the darkened waters,
Moving like sunrise over the unviewed waste,
Before the waking Hesperus and his daughters
Sang by their tree the golden apples' taste,
We were alive upon the evening roof
Seeing the gay lights from glittering ships,
Still and aware, unseparate and aloof,
Musicked by summer into time's eclipse,
And we shall yet be there
When light is dark, and the last tree of spring blown bare.

All of true love, the passion and compassion,
The quenchless pity, the untrammelled pride,
The knowledge whence divided lovers fashion
Their bread of life—the body's bread denied,
The dear affection, the surpassing peace,
The friendship that is daylight in the soul,
The body's ardour, and the mind's release,
Love, that alone makes man entire and whole,
Quiet, and intent, and gay,
The calm celestial dullness of love's day-to-day—

This is the fortress centuries cannot storm,
These are the lifted gates of David's story,
Shut fast against the insurgent minutes' swarm,

Flung open to receive the King of Glory;
This is the native element of man,
This climate of content and sudden laughter,
Whilst angry aeons fret their sluggard span,
This was before, this is for ever after—
Though time's malign misprision
Darkens and separates and dulls the mortal vision.

Love is a moving onwards, an invasion
Into a land whose limits are unset,
A transit, and a torrent, a persuasion
That what must come excels what has been yet.
Ache not for beauty's flight, who shall surprise
A joy that our unwisdom cannot measure,
Love is an unfulfilment, a surmise,
The awaken'd heart travelling towards its treasure.
Arise, and as he shone
Shine too; love is an iron compulsion to be on.

Love is a paradox, a stream afire,
A fusion and diffusion of the heart,
Whose sweet confederacy can still aspire
Towards that throne of which it is a part.
Love is a faith, a darling death to life,
A blessedness wherein true virtue lies,
A glowing dark, a peace in constant strife,
The stillness of a ceaseless exercise:
An ignorance of sin,
The God without us summoning the God within.

Love is an electricity, a flame
Sequestered from the sizeless vault of light,
An impetus, that men a little tame
And use amidst uncomprehending night;

Infinite violence from the powers that spin
Their spiral galaxies through volted space,
Tremendously and bravely worn within
This minimum and mortal carapace
The body's brittle cage,
Charged with the lightning's wild unharnessable rage.

Unsentimental God designs our plight,
Regarding with long love and long derision
Our baby rage and buffetings, our slight
And brief accords; with adamant precision
Numbers our hairs and knows the tumbling sparrows;
Insufferable upon love's giant span
Shoots his astonishing unwayward arrows
And lets us make what sense of it we can,
Learn or despair, and grow
Plodding or swift towards the stature we shall know.

His mind conceives the mandrill, and the lion,
And sends quadruplets to the bishop's wife;
He sees the children bleed, he flung Orion
In Heaven's arch; he jars the surgeon's knife,
And with an intricate and equal hand
Unfolds the cancer, and unfolds the rose,
And breathes the spring like flame along the land;
He is the wind of death when phosgene blows
Across the topless city,
An iron compassionate love that never bends to pity.

Free will, and Heaven's order, both are true,
Life's sheet is pencilled in, and ours the choice
To paint in flaming or sepulchral hue,
Sad indigoes, vermilions that rejoice
The rainbow incoherence of our youth,

The cloudy umber, or the deep cobalt,
Ours the selection of our only truth,
Drabs that debase or splendours that exalt;
The choice is freely given
Though the whole scene was painted long ago in Heaven.

Enslaved, we wear the despot's diadem;
Free and withheld, its way the spirit keeps,
The waters move and swell and we in them
Through sparkling shallows and untroubled deeps.
Life unbecalmed, unshipwrecked, never spent,
By devious passage to one harbour driven,
Is borne to where the tide of God's intent
Drawn by the vast and mellowing moon of Heaven,
Breaks in a long refrain
On shores where joy and sorrow thunder their twin
    strain.

On shores where manhood's questing footsteps tread
Eternally with life and vision shod,
A light-apparelled country where outspread
The limitless imaginings of God.
Love, whose far-travelled light is all our shining,
Ray round the human heavens with your glow,
In all refulgence and all power inclining
Our beings to that journey they must go,
Till we, waking on earth,
May live, moving towards God in everlasting birth.